KITTEN CA

FOR CHILDREN

by
GRACE McHATTIE

Photographs by Grace McHattie
assisted by Gordon McHattie

ANDRE DEUTSCH

The author would like to thank Peter Burgess, MA, VetMB, MRCVS, and everyone else who appeared in the *Kitten Care for Children* photographs, especially her Ragdoll cat, Crystal, and Crystal's three kittens, Gemini, Andromeda and Aqua.

First published in 1989 by
André Deutsch Limited
105–106 Great Russell Street, London WC1B 3LJ

Text and photographs copyright © 1989 Grace McHattie
ISBN hardback 0 233 98400 3
ISBN paperback 0 233 98426 7

Phototypeset by AKM Associates (UK) Ltd
Ajmal House, Hayes Road, Southall
Printed in Spain by Printek, Bilbao

Contents

The First Eight Weeks

The first eight weeks in a kitten's life are the most important. How the kitten has been treated during those eight weeks will affect how it will behave for the rest of its life.

If the mother cat has given birth to her litter in a hidden place and the kittens don't see any people for the first two months of their lives, they will never be very friendly towards people and may even be frightened by them.

By the time a kitten is eight weeks old, it has grown as much as a child of three years. Kittens mature and grow much faster than children. It only takes one week for a new-born kitten to double its weight; it takes a human baby five or six months to double its birthweight.

A kitten weighs about 925 grams to 1375 grams (two to three ounces) when it is born. It is unable to open its eyes. It cannot walk, but can crawl on its stomach to find its mother – and her milk – which it finds by smell and the sound of the mother cat's purring. A new-born kitten has no teeth and, although it has claws, it is unable to retract them into the sheaths in its paws as a cat can.

The kitten's mother will have found a quiet, private place to give birth and to raise her kittens. Once an owner has checked that the kittens are fit and well, mother and babies should be left in peace, and not disturbed more than necessary.

In a kitten's first few days, any time not spent nursing from its mother is spent sleeping, curled up with its mother keeping it warm, or lying in a heap with all the other kittens in the litter. A kitten's mother will do everything for it for the first month of life, not only feeding it her milk but groom-

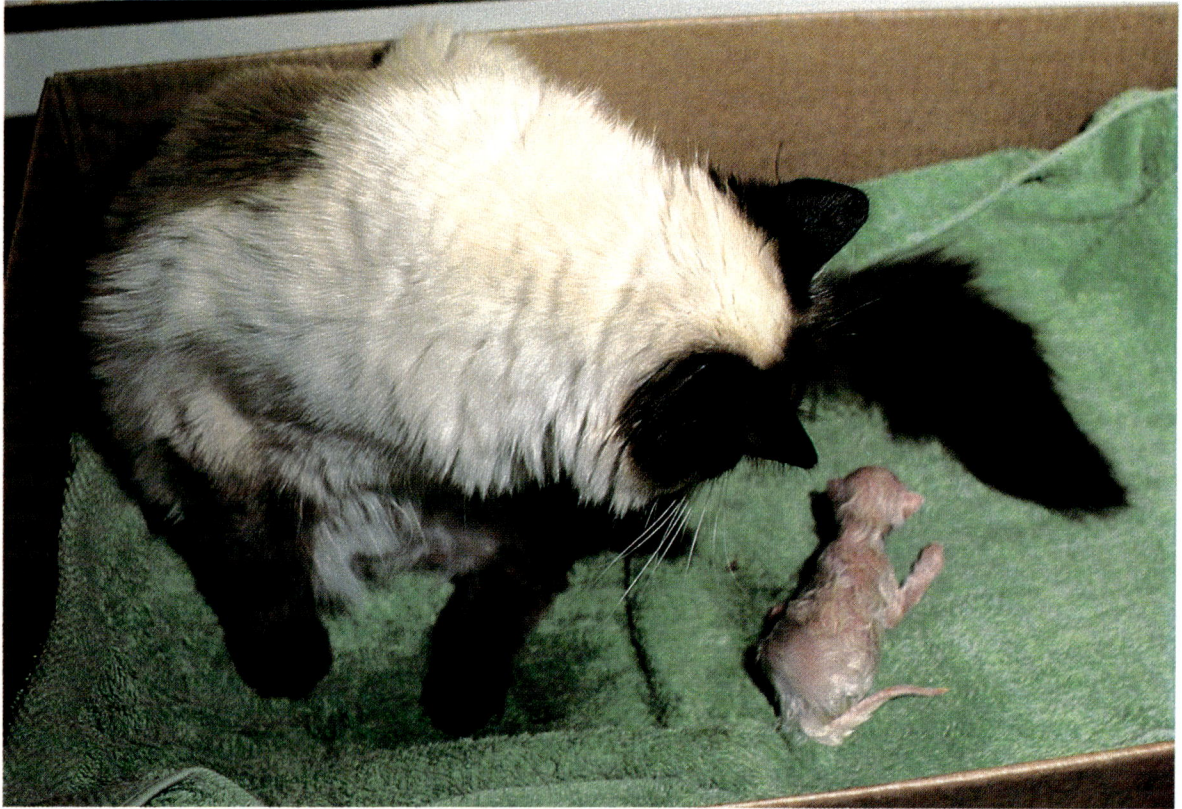

The first kitten has just been born. Its fur is still damp.

ing it too. After a meal, she will lick the kitten from top to bottom, not only cleaning it but also encouraging it to get rid of its waste products. It cannot do this by itself for about four weeks!

After the first few days, the kitten's umbilical cord (through which it was nourished in its mother's womb) has dried up and dropped off. This leaves a little

tummy button which is hidden when the fur grows thicker. All kittens (and cats) have nipples too – eight of them – whether they are male or female, but these usually can't be seen because of the fur.

By the fifth day, the kitten will purr when its mother is feeding it. Kittens usually choose their 'own' teat from which to feed and will use the same one each time. While feeding, a kitten will press both sides of the teat continuously. This is called 'kneading' and will help the milk flow. Many kittens continue the kneading movement all through their lives when they feel happy, (for example, when they are about to sit down on your lap) as it is connected in their minds with the pleasure of being fed.

By the tenth day, the kitten's eyes will be opening, although it won't be able to see much. All kittens' eyes are blue at this age. Although a few breeds of pedigree cats have blue eyes, most kittens' eyes will later change colour to gold or green.

If it is startled, a ten-day old kitten will hiss, although it is otherwise unable to defend itself. Its first, milk teeth are beginning to develop but they are very tiny indeed!

The dry kittens are 15 and 30 minutes old. The third kitten is just a few minutes old and still wet but all three are feeding.

These kittens are five days old. Their eyes are still closed and they are huddling together for warmth. Although these kittens were born white, their ears are now beginning to change colour.

The kittens are now ten days old and their eyes are beginning to open. Their ears have become darker and the nose of one of the kittens is beginning to turn brown.

Between ten days and three weeks, a kitten will start to explore. Although it still cannot walk, its legs are strong enough for it to push itself upright. If it is living in a kittening box, it will try to climb out. It will also start to touch objects which interest it, with its paw. More kittens are 'left-pawed' than 'right-pawed' and will use their left front paw most often to touch anything of interest.

By the age of three weeks, a litter of kittens will be beginning to play. Over the next week, the kitten will learn to do much more than feed and sleep, which is all it

One month old and the kittens are becoming more independent. They weigh four times their birth weight. This kitten is learning to hunt by chasing its mother's tail.

has done up to this time. It will become stronger, will walk well, and be more steady on its feet. It will play with other kittens in the litter, tumbling over them and biting them. Although these are playfights, they will teach the kitten how to defend itself. The kitten will also learn to hunt at this age – by chasing its mother's waving tail!

By the time a kitten is four weeks old, it will be grooming itself, climbing out of its kittening box, using a litter tray by itself, and will be eating some solid food.

Most kittens will still try to get milk from their mothers. However, at some time between four and eight weeks, their mother will start to get bored with feeding them, and will run away from her kittens!

Some kittens mature faster than others. Pedigree kittens will usually go to their new homes at the age of 12 weeks. Non-pedigree kittens, which grow up more quickly, are usually ready to move on at the age of eight weeks or so.

Pedigree or non-pedigree?

Pedigree kittens are kittens of a particular 'breed'. Generally speaking, all cats of one breed will look alike. A pedigree kitten's parents, grandparents, great-grandparents and great-great-grandparents will be known and their names will appear on a pedigree certificate, which is a piece of paper which you will be given when you buy a pedigree kitten. A pedigree kitten will cost much more than a non-pedigree kitten. A non-pedigree kitten often won't look like its parents and its ancestry isn't known. Both types of kittens make good pets – it just depends on what you're looking for.

Choosing Your Kitten

When you hear about kittens for sale, look at them with the intention of *looking* rather than *buying*. The first kittens you see may not be suitable.

Don't be afraid to inspect a kitten (or cat) carefully before you buy it. You should always make sure that the kitten is healthy.

It should look healthy and happy and it should not be nervous of people. Unless it is asleep when you arrive, it should be curious when it sees you and come to look at you.

Pick it up and look at it closely. Its eyes should be open and bright and it shouldn't have any signs of runny or weepy eyes. Its nose should also be clean and not runny and it should not be sneezing. If its eyes look sore or it is sneezing, do not buy it. It could have a serious (even fatal) illness which it might pass on to any other cats you may have.

Look inside its ears. They should be clean and should not smell (sniff!) If the kitten is scratching its ears, it may have an ear infection. Look in its mouth. Its gums should be pink, not red and sore-looking.

Its fur should be clean and not tangled. Part its fur so you can see its skin. If you find any black specks on the skin, the kitten may have fleas.

The kitten should feel solid and should not appear boney. If it has a round, tight tummy it may have worms.

Lift up its tail and look at its bottom, which should also be quite clean. If the fur around its bottom is matted or is yellowish, the kitten may have diarrhoea. This may just be a sign of a tummy upset, but it might be a symptom of a serious illness.

Kittens should have clear bright eyes – just like this one.

If you are looking at a kitten but aren't sure about its health, you can ask the owner if they will let you take it to a vet, for a check-up, before you buy it. Anyone selling a healthy kitten will have no objections to this, although you will have to pay the vet's bill whether you buy the kitten or not.

If you think there is any possibility the kitten is unwell, *do not buy it*. So if the owner says that the kitten 'just has a tummy upset' or 'has hurt its eye' tell them you'll come back in a couple of days when the kitten is better to have a look at it again. If you buy a sick kitten, it will cost a lot of money in vet's fees; it might make other cats ill if it comes into contact with them; and it might even die.

Always inspect a kitten carefully before you buy it.

You should, if you can, go to see several litters of kittens – that way, you'll know what healthy kittens look like.

Don't rush into buying a kitten. Although it is difficult to say no when you're looking at a cute little ball of fluff, do think seriously about it and remember the kitten will grow up quickly and could be living with you for the next 15–18 years.

You should, if you can, go to see several litters of kittens before making your choice. That way, you will know what a healthy kitten looks like – and what an unhealthy kitten looks like.

If you have a friend whose cat has had kittens, this is often a good way to find a pet. Have a look at the mother cat too, to make sure she looks contented and healthy.

You might find a kitten in one of the many charity-run cats' homes throughout the country, so try telephoning your nearest cats' shelter.

If you're looking for a pedigree kitten, buy a cat magazine to read the breeders' advertisements and visit some cat shows to find out who are the good breeders and who are not. Don't be afraid to ask around – everyone loves giving advice!

Whether pedigree or non-pedigree, think twice or even three times before buying a kitten from a pet store. Pet store kittens are sometimes kept incorrectly, they may be unwell, and the assistants usually know very little about the kittens' mother and the sort of home they came from.

Are you sure . . .?

. . . you will be able to look after your kitten or cat for the next 15 years or so?

. . . you can afford to feed it properly and take it to the vet's, when necessary?

. . . you have provided everything your kitten will need *before* you bring it home?

Taking Your Kitten Home

When you have chosen your kitten, you will need a secure cat carrier in which to take it home. Even if you are travelling by car, it is very dangerous to try to carry your kitten, as kittens are very good at wriggling out of people's arms, and they can end up under the car's pedals, causing an accident.

You will need a cat carrier many times, for visits to the vet and so on, so buy a good one to start with and it will last for your cat's lifetime. You can buy one from most pet stores. Carrying kittens or cats in cardboard boxes is not a good idea as they may become frightened and rip their way out of them.

Let your kitten explore the open carrier before you put it into it, so that it will not be frightened.

If you are being driven home, ask to be driven slowly and carefully, so that the kitten isn't shaken about in the carrier.

Your new kitten will be happier if, at first, your home is quiet and peaceful. Although you will have lots of friends who will want to see your kitten, ask them to wait for a few days until the kitten has settled down. It is not a good idea to bring a kitten into your home if a birthday party is taking place or during the Christmas period. The kitten will take a few days to get used to its new home and it will be upset by a lot of noise, disruption, or strangers. Your kitten will also want to sleep a lot while it is young – maybe as much as 18 or 20 hours a day.

Before letting it out of its carrier, make sure the windows are closed, fireplaces are blocked off (a nervous kitten will often run straight up a chimney!) precious ornaments are put out of reach, and

Young kittens are very active and need lots of sleep sometimes 18 hours a day or more.

there is nothing dangerous which a kitten can chew or choke on.

Then let your kitten out, but keep it in one room at first. Show it where its litter tray and feeding bowls are, and don't move these for a few days. Kittens are usually house-trained and will use their litter tray but, if your kitten uses the floor as a toilet, don't shout at it or smack it. It may just be confused, or have a tummy upset because it is nervous about its change of home. You could help by placing it on its tray an hour or so after every meal, so it learns what is expected of it.

Ask the person you bought the kitten from what it has been eating and continue to feed the same food for a while. If you want to change its food, do so gradually, mixing in a little of the new food with the food it has been used to. If you change its food too rapidly, it may suffer a tummy upset.

Kittens love to play and chase dangled ribbons. Make sure you hold the other end securely – if a kitten starts to swallow a ribbon, it cannot spit it out. Never leave your kitten alone to play with string or wool.

Remember that kittens are adventurous and can easily get into danger. This kitten has climbed up the chimney because the fireplace was not blocked off.

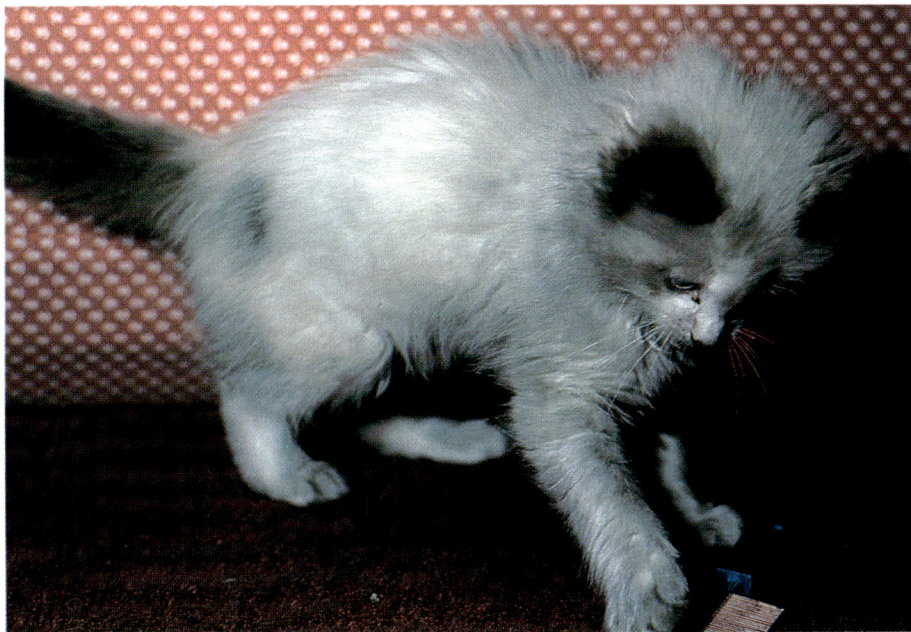

Don't allow your kitten out of doors at first as it may become lost or get into danger. It shouldn't go out of doors until a week or so after it has been protected by injections (vaccinations) from your vet as it could become ill if it comes into contact with a sick cat.

While your cat is still a kitten, get it used to staying indoors at night. Cats should never be 'put out' at night as they are more likely to be stolen or run over during the hours of darkness.

Remember that kittens are adventurous and can easily get into danger. Always check washing-machines and other appliances before switching them on – your kitten may be inside. A kitten may chew wires, so keep wires out of reach if you can, or unplug electrical appliances when they're not being used. Keep toilet lids down – young kittens can fall inside and be unable to get out again!

If you already have a cat or a dog, introduce the two very carefully so they can become friends. If you have a dog, keep it under control, perhaps on its lead, while the two introduce themselves. Don't allow your dog to bark or to run at the kitten – and be careful your kitten doesn't scratch your dog's face!

If you already have a cat, you must ignore your kitten at first (difficult though that is) until your cat makes friends with it. If you make a big fuss of your kitten and ignore your cat, it may become jealous and never like the new kitten. Although your cat and kitten will hiss at each other and fight at first, they should settle down together within a few days, as long as you leave them to sort it out between them. Do make sure there is somewhere in the room for your kitten to hide if your cat is being rough with it – an empty cardboard box is ideal.

And do make sure your kitten has its own bed (a clean cardboard box with a blanket is fine) and its own food and water bowls. If you have a cat already, it won't want to share its bed or food with the newcomer!

Your kitten will need a comfortable bed, a litter tray and a scratching post to keep its claws in shape.

What your kitten will need

A warm, comfortable bed, out of any draughts

A bowl for food and one for water, and a supply of food

Litter in a litter tray, which should be cleaned out regularly

A few safe toys to play with

A quiet, peaceful place to live, at least for the first few days

A cat carrier and, if possible, a scratching post

A vet – ask your friends to recommend a good one *before* you bring your kitten home. Keep your vet's number beside the telephone.

Once you become a cat-owner, you will need the help of a vet from time to time. It's a good idea to have your kitten checked over by a vet as soon as you buy it (or even before you buy it). Your vet will check that the kitten is strong and healthy; will listen to its heart through a stethoscope; will check its ears, eyes and body, and may give it a worming tablet, if necessary.

Your vet will also recommend that your kitten should be vaccinated against two fatal illnesses at the age of around nine weeks. A second vaccination will be given at about 12 weeks and yearly 'booster' vaccinations will be given for the rest of your cat's life.

These vaccinations will help protect your kitten or cat against a disease called *panleucopaenia*, which causes vomiting and diarrhoea, and against respiratory infections. Respiratory infections are often referred to as cat 'flu, but cat 'flu is much more serious for a cat than human 'flu is to a human. Respiratory infections cause sneezing with running eyes and noses. These illnesses can kill cats and kittens which are not protected by vaccination.

It will take about a week after the second vaccination before your kitten is fully protected against these illnesses, so do not allow it out of doors until then.

While at the veterinary surgery, you can also discuss neutering or spaying. Spaying a female kitten will prevent it having kittens when it gets older. Spaying is carried out under anaesthetic, while your kitten is 'asleep' and will not hurt your pet (in fact, having kittens is likely to hurt her much more!)

There are already more pet kittens and cats than there are homes for, so many kittens are destroyed each year.

Your vet will advise you of the best time for the operation. For female kittens this will be around five to six months and, for male kittens, neutering will be carried out between four to nine months.

Neutering of male kittens will also help stop unwanted kittens being born – and it makes a cat much more pleasant to live with! Male cats which have *not* been neutered have a strong-smelling urine which they spray everywhere, including all over your home. They also get into fights and wander off for days on end looking for female cats to mate with. Male cats don't think they are missing anything once they have been neutered; they are quite content with the new state of affairs.

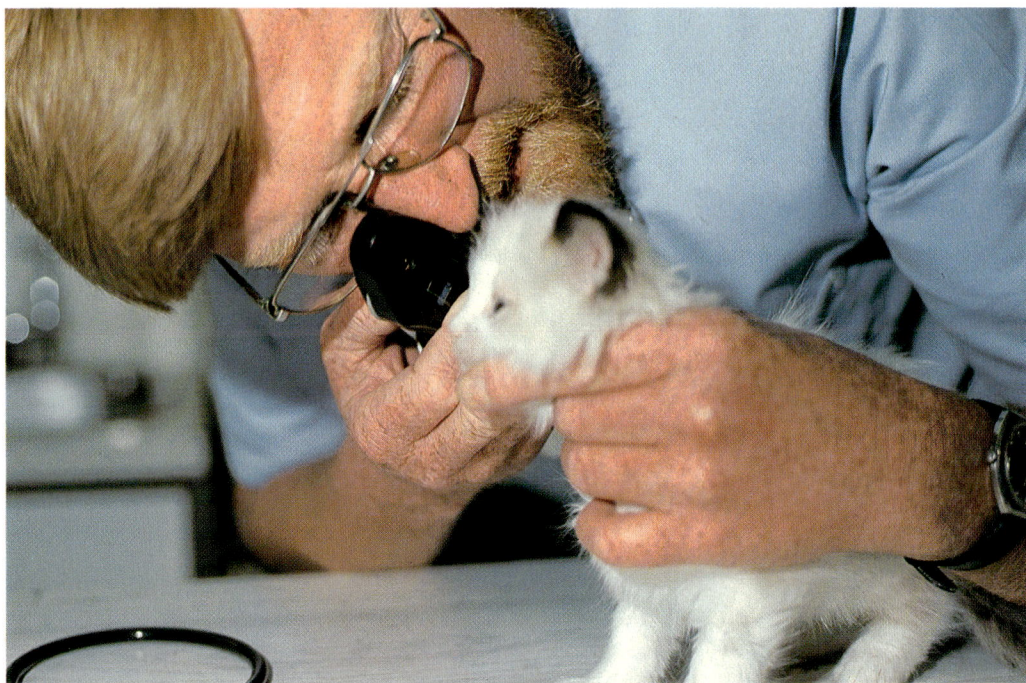

A nine weeks, kittens should visit the vet for their first vaccination. They will also be given a health checkup. This kitten is having its eyes checked with an ophthalmoscope.

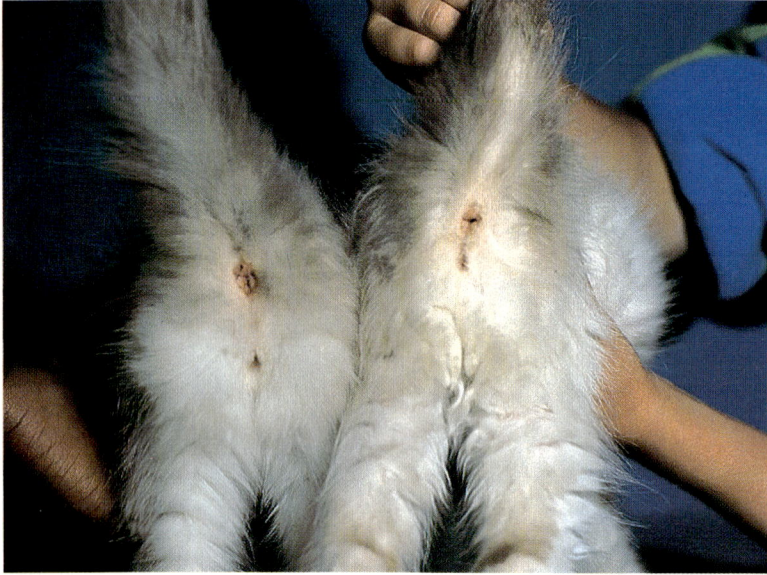

How to tell if your kitten is male or female. The male is on the left. The two openings are further apart than in the female on the right.

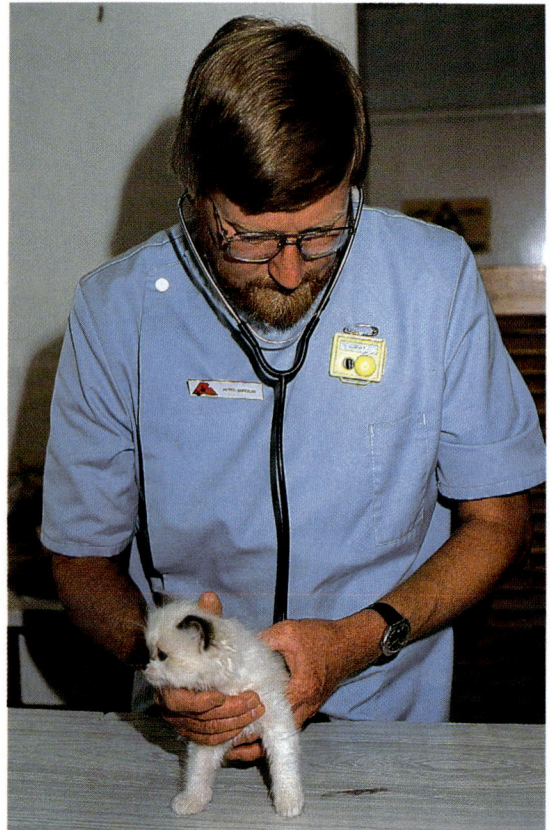

This kitten's heart is being listened to with a stethoscope.

It isn't true that neutered cats become fat. Nor does neutering make them unhappy. In fact, neutered cats live longer than cats which have not been neutered because they don't get into so many fights (if male) or face the risks of kitten-birth (if female).

Some people think that cats should have one litter of kittens 'for their health' before they are spayed, but this is nonsense. Having a litter of kittens does not help a cat and may even harm it.

As well as giving your kitten a health check-up and neutering it when it is old enough, your vet will look after your cat if it becomes ill or is injured. If you find it difficult to budget for illness or injury, you can take out health insurance for your pet. You will have to pay a certain amount for the insurance each month, then, if your kitten becomes ill or is injured, the insurance company will pay the vet's fees. (Insurance does not cover the cost of the yearly vaccinations or the cost of neutering). Your vet will give you information about health insurance.

Danger!

Don't ever give your cat pain-killers. Aspirin and paracetomol can kill a cat.

If your cat cuts itself and the cut is not deep, wash the wound in warm water with a little salt in it. Don't use antiseptics or disinfectant – many are very poisonous to cats.

If your cat starts to vomit, has diarrhoea, fits, or staggers around, it may have been poisoned. Don't give it anything to make it sick – you may make matters worse. Place it in a dark, quiet place and immediately telephone your vet.

If ever in doubt about your cat's health, telephone your vet. The vet or veterinary assistant may be able to advise you by telephone – or they may recommend that you bring your cat to the surgery.

Feeding Your Kitten

Young kittens can't eat very much at one time, so should be fed several times a day. When you buy your kitten at eight to twelve weeks of age, it should be fed four times a day. When it is four to six months old, it can have three meals a day and when it reaches eight months, feed it twice a day. It's a good idea to feed your kitten its last meal of the day in the late evening; if your kitten goes out of doors during the day, this will ensure it comes in for the night.

Good-quality tinned foods are specially made for cats and are very nourishing. Few people nowadays cook food specially for their cats. Choose a tinned food which is high in protein and low in ash content (read the labels). The most expensive food isn't always the best! The makers of pet foods should recommend how much to feed your kitten or cat on the labels. Be careful not to overfeed.

While your cat is still a kitten, it needs a high-protein diet, and there are tinned foods specifically made for kittens which you can buy from your pet store. Don't feed kittens dry food, but adult cats can be given a little to exercise their teeth.

However, dry food *is* dry and cats need moisture. Many cats don't drink extra liquid when they are given dry food and this can lead to problems with your cat's health. So if you give your cat dry food, limit it to just a few pieces each day.

Make sure your kitten is used to different types of food from an early age so it doesn't become fussy, and don't allow it to insist on one type of food only.

Some cats like liver so much they refuse to eat anything else. So you should not give your cat or

Kittens should always have their own feeding bowl – although they might choose to share! These are not the best bowls to use as they should be wider and shallower.

kitten liver more than once a week or so. Too much liver will make your cat ill from an overdose of Vitamin A. A diet of fatty fish such as canned sardines or mackerel will result in your cat not receiving enough Vitamin E and will make it ill. If you feed fish to your cat, it should always be cooked, as it is more nourishing than raw fish.

Cats and kittens should not be fed dog food on a regular basis. Dog food is lacking in a substance called *taurine* which a cat needs in its diet (a dog doesn't) and, without it, a cat will go blind. For the same reason, a cat will go blind if fed on a completely vegetarian diet.

As well as tinned food, and a little dry food, you can give your cat nourishing leftovers, such as the dark meat and skin from chickens or fowl, cooked, trimmed fat from cutlets, a little hard cheese, and cooked egg (never give a cat raw egg white).

Kittens, once they have left their mothers, do not need milk. In fact, many cats and kittens are allergic to milk and it will give them diarrhoea.

All cats and kittens *do* need water and they should always have a clean, fresh bowl of water available, even if you never see them drinking from it!

Food facts

Cats don't like cold food so don't give them a meal which has just come out of the refrigerator. Microwave ovens are very useful for warming food up.

Cats like a quiet place to eat – somewhere they don't run the risk of being tripped over. Some cats don't like their food bowl to be placed near their litter tray.

If you have more than one cat, each should have its own feeding bowl.

Bowls should be washed regularly as a cat will not use a smelly or dirty bowl. Bowls should be wider than a cat's whiskers. If the bowl is too narrow, your cat may trail the food onto the floor to eat it.

Keeping Your Kitten Healthy

How do you know if your kitten is ill?

If your kitten . . .

. . . coughs or sneezes and has runny eyes or nose

. . . or its third eyelid (at the inside corner of its eye) is showing, or there is a film over its eye

. . . or it is straining in its litter tray but is unable to pass anything, or it appears constipated

. . . or it is passing urine or faeces with blood in it

. . . or it is urinating very frequently

. . . or it is vomiting or has diarrhoea for more than 24 hours

. . . or it is excessively thirsty

. . . or it is drooling, or frothing at the mouth

. . . or it is staggering, paralysed, or having a fit

. . . or its breathing becomes difficult

. . . or it constantly scratches its ears

. . . or it has any swellings, heavily-bleeding wounds or appears to be in pain

. . . or if you're just worried about your kitten's health . . .

CONTACT YOUR VET IMMEDIATELY

Grooming

Although cats groom themselves by licking their fur, it will help keep your kitten healthy if you comb it at least once a week with a metal cat comb. In the spring, when your kitten is moulting, you should comb it several times a week. However, if you have a longhaired kitten such as a Persian, it must be combed every day or its coat will become tangled and matted.

This will not only help stop cat hair going all over the furniture, but it will stop your kitten from swallowing the fur, which can collect into a ball in its stomach. If your kitten has a furball, it may seem off-colour and not want to eat. You can buy a furball treatment from your pet store, but follow directions very carefully and, if the furball is not expelled within 24 hours, contact your vet.

Comb your kitten carefully at least once a week using a special metal cat comb.

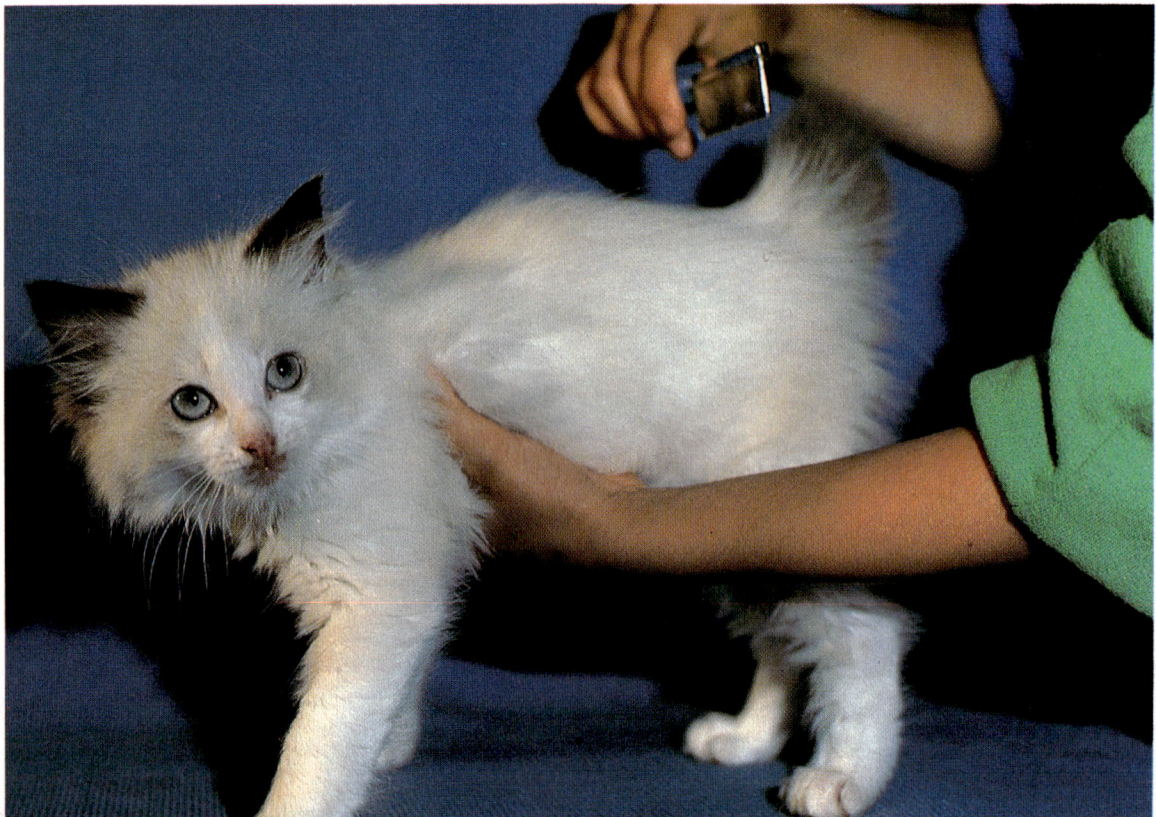

Start grooming your kitten when it is young so that it becomes used to it. Start by simply running your hands over its fur in a grooming motion, then, when it is used to that, use the comb gently.

When you groom your kitten, check if its ears are clean. If not, they should be cleaned very gently with a cotton bud, holding it vertical and *not* pushing down into the ear canal or it will hurt your kitten. This is rather tricky, so you might like to ask a grown-up to do it for you.

Fleas

When you groom your kitten, you might see some little black specks in its fur, or you might notice your cat scratching itself. These are signs of fleas.

Some people are upset when they find their cat has fleas but *all* cats have fleas at some time or other; it doesn't mean they are dirty or uncared for! However, you should treat your kitten's fleas as soon as possible.

You can buy flea spray from a vet or pet store and it's probably a

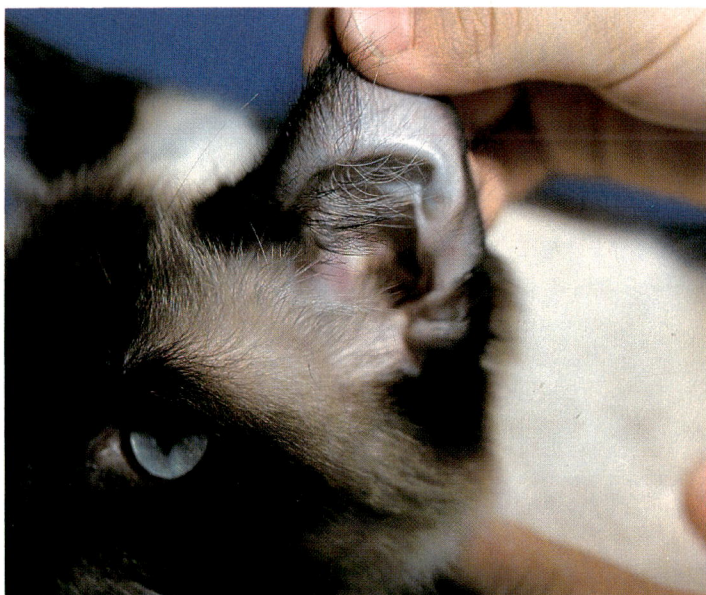

Check that your kitten's ears are clean and that there is no wax or sign of infection in the ear.

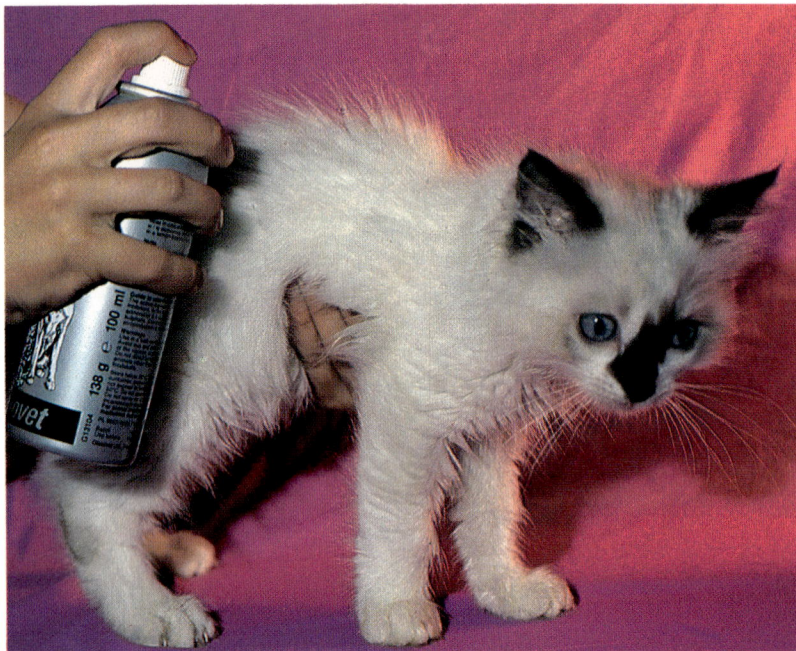

Spray your kitten carefully if you see signs of fleas. Be sure to read the instructions on the can carefully before you begin.

good idea to ask a grown-up to spray your kitten as kittens don't like it! If your kitten is still young, make sure you buy a spray suitable for young kittens; a spray for adult cats may be too strong for it and make it very ill.

Follow the instructions on the can *very* carefully and don't spray the contents over your kitten's face. Don't spray your kitten in the same room as its food or water bowls (or in the same room as a fish tank – it can poison the fish).

At the time, you should spray your home with a special flea treatment (from your vet or pet store) which will kill any fleas in furniture or carpets, where they breed. Never use this sort of spray on your kitten's fur – only on furniture and carpets.

Try not to breathe in any flea spray while spraying your kitten and always wash your hands afterwards.

Don't use flea collars, if you can help it, as your kitten will have flea poison in contact with its skin at all times, which may cause a rash on its neck. If you do use one, take it off from time to time to allow your kitten's neck to 'breathe'. A flea collar will not begin to work until a few days after you have placed it on your kitten.

Worms

Kittens can be born with worms and they can become infected by swallowing a flea or eating a mouse with worm eggs in its system. Worms live in a cat's bowel and you may not know they're there. So buy worming tablets from your vet or pet store and use them regularly; as often as is recommended on the packet.

Don't overdose your kitten or cat though, as this can make them very sick indeed. And don't give your kitten or cat a worming tablet at the same time as using a flea treatment on it. The two treatments used together can be toxic – wait a few days. If your kitten has a fat, round tummy, its fur looks rough and not shining, it loses weight, coughs, is restless, or even has diarrhoea or vomits, it may have worms.

Many worming tablets now are 'palatable'. This means that your kitten will eat them as if they are treats, or they can be crushed up and mixed with its food.

If you have to give your kitten a pill, again, ask a grown-up for help. The kitten should be held gently but firmly between the knees, its mouth opened and tilted back, and the pill dropped into the back of its mouth. Hold its mouth closed while its throat is gently stroked, which will make it swallow the tablet. Make sure you aren't covering its nose or it won't be able to breathe.

Remember to wash your hands every time you handle a cat or kitten, especially if you've been worming it, treating it with flea spray or cleaning out its litter tray.

Living with your kitten

Your kitten won't always be a kitten and it will change as it gets older. At first, it will be very playful and probably a bit naughty. You should gently train it to fit into your household by saying a firm 'no' and removing it from anything which it shouldn't be doing.

It will become an adult around the age of one year or so. It will still enjoy playing with you from time to time, although now it may think it is your boss!

As your cat gets older, it will slow down and be more of a lap cat. It will enjoy sleeping in the sun and in warm places. It will appreciate your assistance with grooming and it needs less protein in its food. You can add some pasta, potatoes or bread to its usual food to keep it healthy. If it has kept fit and well, it will still enjoy some gentle play.

Whatever age your pet is, whether kitten, cat or pensioner puss, it will be your friend all its life. Look after your friend well and it will reward you with its love and companionship.